MOTOWN
ANTHOLOGY

ISBN 0-7935-9201-1

HAL•LEONARD®
CORPORATION
7777 W. BLUEMOUND RD. P.O. BOX 13819 MILWAUKEE, WI 53213

Visit Hal Leonard Online at
www.halleonard.com

Contents

Contents

The Motown Story

by Mark Etzkorn

In 1965, if you wanted to send a fan letter to your favorite singer at your favorite record company, you might have addressed the envelope to Hitsville, U.S.A. It probably would have landed correctly at Motown headquarters in Detroit.

That title, adorning an unimposing frame house on Grand Boulevard that served as Motown's headquarters, was not an idle boast. By the mid-1960s, the company was a true music industry colossus, an instantly recognizable brand name responsible for some of the most successful — and most memorable — pop music of that or any other era. As song after song by Smokey Robinson and The Miracles, The Marvelettes, Mary Wells, Martha and The Vandellas, The Temptations, The Supremes, The Four Tops, Marvin Gaye, Stevie Wonder, The

Berry Gordy

Jackson 5, and others shot up the charts, Motown cemented its reputation as *the* purveyor of exciting, impeccably crafted, expertly executed pop-soul music — songs that left an indelible mark on audiences around the world.

The Motown releases of the 1960s and early 1970s — "Money (That's What I Want)," "Shop Around," "Dancing in the Street," "I Heard It through the Grapevine," "My Girl," "Where Did Our Love Go?" "I Can't Help Myself," "Ain't Too Proud to Beg," "I Want You Back," to name a only a handful — are more than pop history; they are part of a vital music vocabulary that continues to inspire performers and delight listeners to this day. These songs represent a body of popular music that has served as the virtual soundtrack for the lives of multiple generation of music fans.

Unlike other songs from the era, the Motown hits do not now sound hopelessly dated. The energy and emotional resonance that separated Motown from its contemporaries also transcends the time barrier, making the songs as fresh and immediate today as they were decades ago — as evidenced by their continual popularity on radio playlists, movie soundtracks, and the repertoires of performers ranging from bar bands to top recording acts. More than one musical group has paid homage to its roots (and sold a few records) by re-recording a Motown single or introducing one into its set list.

Almost as fascinating as the music itself is the company that made it. An independent, African-American-owned and operated company featuring black performers, Motown bucked the odds — and the times — by selling millions of soul-tinged pop records (or were they pop-tinged soul records?) to a multiracial audience. The Motown era — the music, the cast of characters, the company's unique work environment — has achieved mythological status over the years. But in this case, the reality lives up to the myth.

Beginnings

The story behind Motown is primarily of one Detroit man's burning ambition, perseverance, and talent. The company's beginnings go back to the late 1950s, when Berry Gordy, Jr. finally caught a break as a songwriter after a few years of scratching at the surface of the music business. It was a pivotal event in a career marked by several fits and starts.

One of eight children, Gordy was born November 28, 1929. He dropped out of high school and went through careers as a boxer and soldier before dipping his toes in musical waters by opening a jazz record store, the 3-D Record Mart, after he got out of the service in 1953. The venture went under in 1955, however, and Gordy moved on to several other jobs, including a stint on the Ford assembly line in Detroit.

In his spare time, Gordy began to write R&B songs and tried to sell them to local performers. He spent the next couple of years writing, recording demos, and promoting his compositions — sending them to magazines, songwriting contests, and record companies — with little to show for it other than a small name for himself within the Detroit music scene.

Everything changed when a song he wrote for Jackie Wilson, "Reet Petite," became a hit for Brunswick Records in 1957. Although he pocketed only $1000 on the project, Gordy fueled his reputation as an up-and-coming songwriter and producer by following up with several other successes for Wilson over the next year or so, including "Lonely Teardrops," the first song Gordy wrote that reached number one on the R&B chart and cracked the top ten on the pop chart.

Gladys Knight & The Pips

At this point in his career, Gordy primarily still sold his compositions to other record labels, who then produced the songs themselves. But Gordy was unsatisfied with the quality of many of the releases and he longed to run his own company — to write, produce, and market his music himself. So in 1959, armed with his modest reputation, the money from his recent songs, and $800 borrowed from his family, Berry Gordy officially launched his new career as an independent record producer.

From the start, Gordy tirelessly scoured Detroit for talent. One of the most important connections he made early on was Smokey Robinson, the lead singer and songwriter for a group called The Miracles. He and Robinson were the heart and soul of the early organization, personally handling almost all the songwriting and production chores. The pair continued to solicit and nurture some of the best songwriting, production, and performing talent in the area, plowing the fields for the incredibly fertile period that was to come.

The Miracles themselves were responsible for the first real chart successes completely owned by Gordy, who continued to sell his increasingly popular songs to other record labels — including tunes by The Miracles, Marv Johnson and future Motown songwriter Eddie Holland — while releasing his first productions on the inaugural Motown label, Tamla. (Motown, Gordy, and Tamla were the principal labels; Soul, V.I.P., and Rare Earth joined the fold by the end of the 1960s.) While Gordy, Robinson, and their skeletal staff scored

The Marvelettes

enough modest successes early on to keep spirits up, the company's ultimate survival was hardly a foregone conclusion in the early part of the decade — Motown was not yet the automatic hit machine it would become. Gordy, however, remained relentless, and constantly exhorted his troops to think big. Everybody pitched in at all levels — sending out records, contacting disc jockeys, etc.

Before long, the commitment paid off. Barrett Strong's "Money (That's What I Want)" was the first solid Motown hit in 1960. The Miracles' "Shop Around," released later the same year, was the first million-seller, reaching number two on the pop chart by January 1961. The Motown era had arrived.

Over the next ten years, Motown would transform itself into the largest independent record company in the world (and the largest business of any kind owned by an African-American), steadily refining a unique assembly line song production process that was as inventive as it was successful. The initial hits by Strong and The Miracles at the beginning of the decade and the explosion of The Jackson 5 in the early 1970s were simply bookends to an unprecedented run of commercial and artistic coups. In the mid-sixties Motown was especially

Mary Wells

ratio" is around ten percent). Fifty-six of those songs were number one on either the pop or R&B charts, and twenty-one topped both. In 1964, when the Beatles began setting some records of their own, Motown released sixty singles, seventy percent of which hit the charts — and nineteen made it to number one. The Supremes alone racked up five *consecutive* number one pop hits starting with "Where Did Our Love Go?" in 1964. In 1966, Motown's hit ratio topped seventy-five percent.

But the numbers, as impressive as they are, don't necessarily tell the whole story. Bobby Vinton's "There! I've Said It Again" and the Dixie Cups' "Chapel of Love" both spent more time at number one in 1964 than the Supremes "Where Did Our Love Go?" Which song of the three sounds freshest today? "Mrs. Brown You've Got a Lovely Daughter" by Herman's Hermits was the fourth most popular song of 1965, while "My Girl" by the Temptations checked in at number seventeen (both reached number one). When was the last time you sat down at the piano and knocked off a few bars of "Mrs. Brown . . . ?"

As the sixties progressed, Motown continued to expand, absorbing rival record labels, and resuscitating the careers of acts (like The Four Tops) who had languished with other record companies before hooking up with Motown's crack songwriting and production corps. (By 1966 the company had one hundred performing acts under contract.) As its chart dominance continued — spearheaded by the songs of Smokey Robinson and the Holland-Dozier-Holland trio, performed by The Supremes, The Four Tops, and The Temptations — Motown appeared to realize its self-declared title as "The Sound of Young America." The roster of artists and staff continued to grow, and although it had taken over six other

The Four Tops

dominant, and the company — more than any other American group or record label — fought toe-to-toe with the British invasion bands on the charts.

The numbers are astounding: Between 1960 and 1970 sixty-seven percent of the singles Motown released hit the charts (the industry standard "hit houses surrounding the original office on Grand Boulevard, Motown was obliged to relocate to downtown Detroit in 1968.

The flood of imitations and re-recordings by many performers of the era testifies to the immediate impact Motown had on the musical landscape. The twin heavyweights of the British invasion, The Beatles and The Rolling Stones, both recorded (and performed) Motown songs throughout their

Martha & The Vandellas

careers — "Please Mr. Postman," "Ain't Too Proud to Beg," "Just My Imagination (Running Away with Me)," among others. Barrett Strong's "Money" is the only song by an outside artist that *both* groups recorded in their entire careers. Very few covers by any group, however, managed to match up to the Motown originals.

In the beginning, Motown always seemed to be a step ahead of the competition. But browsing through the Motown releases of the period, one notices a subtle change in both the compositions and their themes. Rawer R&B songs (like The Contours' dance-party smash "Do You Love Me?") and early rock vocal harmony style (such as The Marvelettes' girl-group-innocent number "Please Mr. Postman") eventually gave way to the polished craftsmanship of the mid-sixties. More experimental songs (especially lyrically) began to crop up towards the end of the decade. Motown came into being during a turbulent period in American history. In the late sixties and early seventies especially, Motown began to reflect (perhaps somewhat belatedly) the social and political undercurrents of the times.

Songs like Marvin Gaye's "What's Going On," The Temptations' "Ball of Confusion" and "Papa Was a Rolling Stone," Edwin Starr's "War," and even "Love Child" by The Supremes were indications that Motown was as much a product of the times as they were an influence upon them.

Everyone becomes strongly attached to some of the music in their lives, and it is sometimes difficult to give a objective account of particular songs when they are wrapped in the warm fuzziness of nostalgia and sentiment. Having said that, is there something tangible or concrete about this music that explains the strong hold it continues to have on our collective psyche?

Keep It Simple

The genius of the songs lies in their simplicity. Most Motown singles of the era used a common verse-chorus (or verse-bridge-chorus) pop song structure — with the occasional short instrumental break or key change after the second chorus that catapulted the tune into its final verse. The songs often began with a quick introduction of the dominant instrumental hook or vocal refrain; the bass and guitar licks kicking off The Temptations' "My Girl," for example, or the whispery chorus opening The Supremes' "Baby Love." But more importantly, what distinguished Motown's songs were the traditional gospel, R&B, and blues elements that were wedded to the pure pop songwriting format. It was a marriage made in heaven.

Marvin Gaye

Gospel harmonies, raucous call-and-response vocals, pulsing bass, staccato guitar licks, and soaring string and horn sections punctuated the songs and gave them an emotional depth and visceral punch that separated them from the competition. The number of Motown singles that scored on both the pop and R&B charts testifies to how potent and fully realized the pop-R&B combination was. That an African-American company was able to mass market songs containing strong doses of what had been commonly classified within the music industry up to that time as "race music" gives an indication of how revolutionary Motown was. The songs were hybrids, but undiluted hybrids.

All the elements came together beautifully in a Motown song: irresistible instrumental hooks, toe-tapping rhythms, unforgettable melodies, sing-along choruses, universal lyrics (celebrating either love, the

Musicians (left to right) Robert White, Danny Turner, crew member Earl Van Dyke, Uriel Jones, James Jamerson

search for love, or lamenting love lost), and always-vital performances by talented stars and a peerless house band — all in a three-minute-or-less package that left you craving for more as the song faded out.

And you always got more. Songs were spun out in innumerable variations, some more a product of Gordy's policy of following up a hit with a quick sound-alike whenever possible (the common practice of the era), while others were inventive rearrangements of specific song structures and harmonies. Martha and The Vandellas' "Quicksand" and "Livewire" were obvious, if spirited, attempts to trade on the success of their original hit "Heatwave." On the other hand, The Supremes "Where Did Our Love Go?" and The Four Tops "I Can't Help Myself," are totally distinct songs with identical underlying harmonic structures and similar melodies.

Motown at Work

The organization that created these songs was about as close to a musical "hit factory" as popular music has produced. Motown (which of course took its name from the Motor City), in fact, liked to brag that the Detroit auto industry wasn't the only successful assembly line in town. Ford, GM, and Chrysler may have produced the classic cars of the period; Motown produced the classic songs.

The company was certainly an anomaly, especially considering the times: a wholly black-owned, independent music company flourishing in an over-whelmingly white, corporate industry (and based light years away from the entertainment capitols of New York and Los Angeles); a highly structured, formula-driven business that nonetheless produced songs of unprecedented emotional range and power.

Gordy's Motown didn't so much break the rules as create new ones. It drew strength from its uniqueness, and was able to turn all the characteristics that set it apart — and which might have been seen as impediments — into advantages. As an independent company with total control over everything from production to publishing, Motown was free from outside artistic or financial influence. Further, its somewhat isolated Detroit location helped Gordy keep his talented songwriters and artists out of the reach of competition which might want to spirit them away.

Gordy, by all accounts a first-rate motivator, strove to create a familial but competitive atmos-phere that maximized the talent of Motown's songwriters and singers. Gordy's control over Motown, down the last detail, was complete (many of his relatives, by the way, were on the company payroll). In addition to the writing and production chores he handled personally, he dictated everything from songwriting style to the choreography and dress of performers. The army of songwriters exe-cuted his wishes in the form of compositions. He was a good judge of talent, and he brought aboard people because he appreciated their individual skills. With the performers he turned the songs into care-fully crafted records. The marketing department packaged the polished Motown sound and image for an eager public. It was all part of one, big process.

The assembly line depiction of Motown is not just a fanciful analogy. Company employees — even artists — punched a time clock at the start of the day. At monthly meetings, everyone had to sing the company's official song, a kind of musical pledge of allegiance written by none other than Smokey Robinson. Gordy pitched his songwriters, producers, and performers against each other in a constant competition to turn out the company's next hit. Every song was designed to hit the charts.

Gordy's tactics apparently worked. Motown staffers seemed to thrive in the close-knit environment, feeding off each others' talent, establishing new partnerships and finding success that had eluded them outside the offices and studios at 2648 West Grand. But despite the company time clock, creativity did not quit for the day at five o'clock. If inspiration struck at 2:00 a.m., then everyone gathered at the office to get a song down while ideas were fresh. The first song The Four Tops cut for Motown was recorded in the wee hours when Motown songwriter Brian Holland bumped into the group at a Temptations performance and mentioned he had a song that might be good for them. Everyone headed over to the studio, and "Baby, I Need Your Loving" was recorded that night.

Hit-making at Motown had become a streamlined process by the mid-sixties. Everybody knew his or her role. To start, one of Motown's songwriters — maybe Smokey Robinson, or the team of Brian Holland, Lamont Dozier, and Eddie Holland (Holland-Dozier-Holland) — would work up a tune. When finished they'd take it to the Motown house band, a collection of some of the best R&B musicians of the period sometimes known as the Funk Brothers. Earl Van Dyke on keyboards, Benny Benjamin on drums, James Jamerson on bass, and Robert White, Joe Messina, and Eddie Willis on guitar, formed the core. They were augmented by a revolving troupe of session players.

After the band (who often recorded more than a song an hour in busy periods) nailed

The Temptations

down the tune and laid down the instrumental tracks, several performers might be brought in to compete for the opportunity to record it, unless the song had been earmarked for a particular artist from the start. What's amazing is that it was all done in Motown's less-than-acoustically-perfect cinderblock studio and a maze of makeshift rehearsal rooms.

Although Motown had several top-notch songwriter/producers, including Berry Gordy himself, Smokey Robinson and the Holland-Dozier-Holland trio accounted for the largest number of the biggest Motown hits. Robinson wrote for The Miracles, of course, and also for acts like Mary Wells and The Temptations, while Holland-Dozier-Holland wrote many of the hits for Martha and The Vandellas, The Supremes and The Four Tops, among others. All the Motown staffers were marvelously versatile. Eddie Holland wasn't just part of a songwriting team, he was a former singer who scored a hit of his own with

The Commodores

The songwriting team of Holland-Dozier-Holland

Motown in 1962 ("Jamie"). Robinson didn't just sing chart-toppers with The Miracles. He wrote and produced hits for others. Barrett Strong, singer of one of the first Motown hits, "Money," was also a writer, responsible for records like The Temptations' "Ball of Confusion (That's What The World Is Today)" with partner Norman Whitfield.

But it is the combination of Holland-Dozier-Holland who remain Motown's most legendary songwriting and production team. In them, the Motown ethos reached its pinnacle. Lamont Dozier and Brian Holland initially worked together with only modest success in the early 1960s. Eddie Holland joined after abandoning his performing career. Beginning with the ebullient "Heatwave" by Martha and The Vandellas in 1963, Holland-Dozier-Holland reeled off twenty-eight more top 20 songs over the next three years, including some of the best-known Motown hits (the trio is responsible for more number one songs than any other non-performing songwriting team in music history). But what might have become a rote process — songwriting by numbers — in the hands of lesser talent, was an always evolving and inventive game for the trio, who shared lyrical, melodic and harmonic responsibilities, then cut demos for the musicians and artists to study. They repeatedly dipped into their bag of musical tricks to come up with songs that were unmistakably Motown, but still distinct entities (remember "Where Did Our Love Go?" and "I Can't Help Myself"?).

The Motown house musicians were probably the least-recognized link in the Motown production chain, but the success of the music is almost inconceivable without them. As salaried musicians, they toiled in relative obscurity behind the scenes at Motown, often playing in their off-hours to small audiences at local clubs. The songwriters laid the track. The band powered the train, imbuing every song that crossed their path with energy and professionalism. Composed mostly of older musicians with jazz backgrounds, years of intense collaboration made the band impeccably tight and endlessly inventive. The sparse, propulsive drumming of Benny Benjamin, and the melodic, elliptical bass lines of James Jamerson, Sr. put an unmistakable imprimatur on the Motown recordings of the era. These musicians also had an incalculable influence on many of Motown's top performers. Stevie Wonder, for one, honed his keyboard and drumming skills under the tutelage of Van Dyke and Benjamin while hanging out in the studio.

The Motown grip on artists extended far beyond the recording studio, however. The company owned its own publishing, management and booking arms — it even had its own "finishing school" that instructed performers how to walk, talk, and dress in a manner that promoted the company's sleek image. In-house music coaches and choreographers put performers through endless rehearsals (closely monitored by the ever-vigilant Gordy), sometimes for months, before an act was unveiled to the public or a record finally released. Nothing was left to chance.

The Supremes

The "Motortown Revues," as they were called in the early days — touring performances by various line-ups of the Motown roster — represented another facet of the Motown marketing strategy. Performances were staged to help promote the company as a whole as much as its individual artists. The tours also provided an education of sorts for performers who found themselves bumping up against the racial barriers of the times, especially in the south — segregated dressing rooms and even separate performances for black and white audiences, and less-than-enthusiastic receptions from local officials.

While Motown actively cultivated a cross-racial mass audience, it was also aware of its position at the forefront of black enterprise and culture. Although it is not well-known, Gordy released Rev. Martin Luther King Jr.'s "I Have A Dream" speech as a single in 1963, and produced three albums of speeches by the slain civil rights leader.

The Legacy

Motown's exponential growth in the sixties could not continue indefinitely, even though to many at the time it must have seemed like it would. The sheltered environment and rigid production system Gordy constructed eventually changed as the company simply outgrew itself and stars and staffers began to seek more control over their work (or greater compensation for it).

Holland-Dozier-Holland left the company in 1968, and Motown relocated to Los Angeles in 1971 as Gordy branched out into other areas of the entertainment industry, most notably movies. His first venture, *Lady Sings the Blues*, earned a best actress nomination for Diana Ross for her portrayal of jazz singer Billie Holiday. Many employees — and performers — did not make the move. Gordy later conceded that, as far as producing music was concerned, the company would have been better off had it stayed in Detroit. The Jackson 5 explosion in 1970-71 (their first single, "I Want You Back" remains one of the best records Motown ever released, and contains one of the greatest bass lines in pop history) was among the last successes of the traditional, original Motown assembly line.

Although the west coast move effectively marked the end of an era at Motown of Detroit, the company hardly disappeared from the charts. The Motown stars continued to score huge successes in the 1970s. Stevie Wonder became one of the biggest

The Jackson 5

acts in the music business, and the Jacksons and Michael Jackson continued to score major hits. The Commodores (Motown's all-time biggest seller) and Lionel Richie both had huge success in the 1970s and '80s, while Diana Ross became a successful solo artist. And Motown stalwart Smokey Robinson continued to write and record hits into the 1980s. When Gordy sold Motown in 1988, the company was worth $61 million. Rick James, DeBarge, and Boyz II Men are some of the other top-sellers Motown introduced to the world in subsequent years, and the label's artist list continues to grow.

The music from the seminal period in the 1960s and '70s, however, remains the core of the Motown catalogue, and is as popular and vibrant today as it was when it was first released. Turn on the radio or TV, go to the movies, or put on one of your favorite CDs. Chances are, you'll soon run into some of that legendary Motown sound.

ABC

Words and Music by ALPHONSO MIZELL, FREDERICK PERREN,
DEKE RICHARDS and BERRY GORDY

With drive

Buh, buh, buh, buh, buh, boo, buh, buh, buh, buh, buh, buh. You

went to school to learn _ girl, things you nev - er, nev - er knew be - fore, like _
Read - ing and writ - ing, 'rith - me - tic are the branch - es of the learn - ing tree. With -

"I" be - fore "E" ex - cept af - ter "C" and why two plus two makes four. Now, now, now _
out the roots of a love ev - 'ry day girl, your ed - u - ca - tion ain't com - plete.

Ain't No Mountain High Enough

Words and Music by NICKOLAS ASHFORD
and VALERIE SIMPSON

Ain't Nothing Like the Real Thing

Words and Music by NICKOLAS ASHFORD
and VALERIE SIMPSON

Ain't Too Proud to Beg

Words and Music by EDWARD HOLLAND
and NORMAN WHITFIELD

2. Now I've heard a cryin' man
   Is half a man with no sense of pride,
   But if I have to cry to keep you,
   I don't mind weepin' if it'll keep you by my side.
   (Chorus)

3. If I have to sleep on your doorstep all night and day
   Just to keep you from walking away,
   Let your friends laugh, even this I can stand,
   'Cause I wanna keep you any way I can.
   (Chorus)

4. Now I've got a love so deep in the pit of my heart,
   And each day it grows more and more,
   I'm not ashamed to call and plead to you, baby,
   If pleading keeps you from walking out that door.
   (Chorus)

Bernadette

Words and Music by BRIAN HOLLAND,
LAMONT DOZIER and EDWARD HOLLAND

Medium Rock

Ber - na-dette,
Ber - na-dette,

peo - ple are search - in' for
they want you be - cause

the kind of love _ that
of the pride _ that it

we pos-sess. _____
gives.

Some go on
But Ber - na-dette,

search-in' their whole life through
I want you be - cause

and nev - er find the love I've found
I need you to live.

in you. _____

Baby I Need Your Lovin'

Words and Music by BRIAN HOLLAND,
LAMONT DOZIER and EDWARD HOLLAND

Baby Love

Words and Music by BRIAN HOLLAND,
EDWARD HOLLAND and LAMONT DOZIER

Ben

Words by DON BLACK
Music by WALTER SCHARF

Dancing in the Street

Words and Music by MARVIN GAYE,
IVY HUNTER and WILLIAM STEVENSON

Call - ing out ___ a round ___ the world, "Are you
in - vi - ta - tion a - cross the na - tion, a

read - y for a brand new beat?" Sum-mer's here, ___ and the
chance _ for the folks to meet. _____ There'll be laugh-ing, _ sing - ing, and

time is right ____ for danc - ing ___ in the streets. _
mu - sic swing - ing and danc - ing ___ in the streets. _

___ They're danc - ing in ___ Chi - ca - go, ___
Phil - a - del - phia P. A., ___

down in New Or - leans, ___
Balt - i - more and D. C., ____ now, ___

D.S. al Coda

They're danc-ing in the __ street. __ Oo. This is an

CODA

danc - ing __ in the street. Yeah. _____

E7

1-3

4

G#

Ah.

Oh, it does-n't mat-ter

Phil - a - del-phia P. A., __
Instrumental - Spoken ad lib. names of cities

Balt - i -more   and D. C. ___   now, __

And if we get __ to that Mo - tor Cit - y,   Ah, __

Repeat and Fade

__ way down __ in L. A., Cal - i - for - ni - a.

Going to a Go-Go

Words and Music by WILLIAM "SMOKEY" ROBINSON, MARVIN TARPLIN,
WARREN MOORE and ROBERT ROGERS

Chorus

Easy

Words and Music by
LIONEL RICHIE

For Once in My Life

Words by RONALD MILLER
Music by ORLANDO MURDEN

62

Got to Be There

Words and Music by
ELLIOTT WILLENSKY

Got to Give It Up

Words and Music by
MARVIN GAYE

Moderate

A7

I used to go out to par - ties _____
stand - in' _____

and _ stand _ a - round; _____
up - side the wall. _____

'cause I was too ner -
I have got _

- vous _____ to real - ly get _ down.
my - self to - geth - er, ba - by, now I'm hav - in' a ball. _____

3. Move your body, move baby, and dance all night,
   To the groovin', I feel all right.
   Havin' a party, ooh, invite all your friends;
   But if you see me stop by, let me in.
   Baby, just party all night long.
   Let me slip into your erotic zone.
   (We heard that!)

(Extra Lyrics for Ad Lib Ending)
Keep on dancin', oh keep on dancin'.
Ooh, look so good, yeah, keep on dancin'.
Oh, now sugar, got to give it up.
Keep on dancin', gotta give it up.
Keep on dancin' . . . .

How Sweet It Is
(To Be Loved by You)

Words and Music by EDWARD HOLLAND,
LAMONT DOZIER and BRIAN HOLLAND

Coda

You were bet-ter to me than I was to my-self, ___ for

me there's_you and there ain't no-bo-dy else. ___I want to stop and thank you

ba - by; ___ I want to stop and thank you ba - by, yes I do,

repeat and fade

How sweet it is ___ to be loved by you.

Heatwave
(Love Is Like a Heatwave)

Words and Music by EDWARD HOLLAND,
LAMONT DOZIER and BRIAN HOLLAND

I Can't Get Next to You

Words and Music by BARRETT STRONG
and NORMAN WHITFIELD

D.%. al Coda

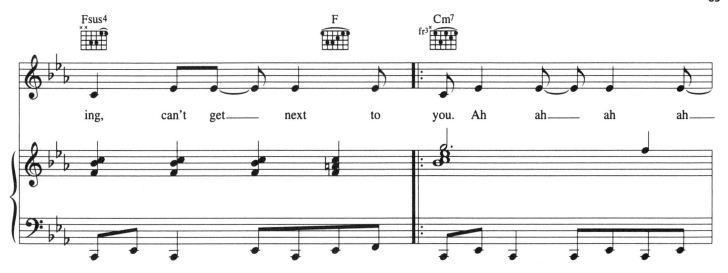

ing,   can't get—— next   to   you. Ah   ah— ah   ah——

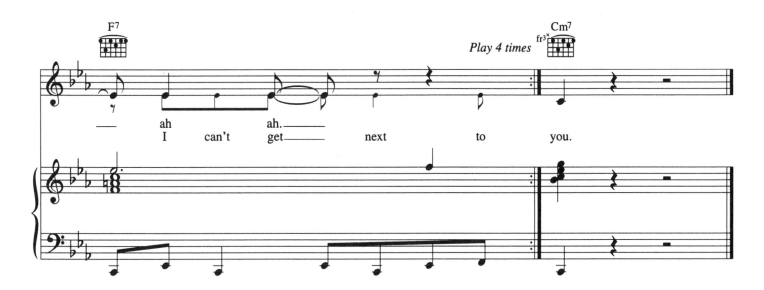

— ah   ah.——

I   can't get—— next   to   you.

Play 4 times

Verse 2:
I can fly like a bird in the sky
And I can buy anything that money can buy.
I can turn a river into a raging fire
I can live forever if I so desire.
I don't want it, all these things I can do
'Cause I can't get next to you.

Verse 3:
I can turn back the hands of time - you better believe I can
I can make the seasons change just by waving my hand.
I can change anything from old to new
The thing I want to do the most I'm unable to do.
I'm an unhappy woman with all the powers I possess
'Cause man, you're the key to my happiness.

I Can't Help Myself
(Sugar Pie, Honey Bunch)

Words and Music by BRIAN HOLLAND,
LAMONT DOZIER and EDWARD HOLLAND

-ter how I try, my love _____ I can - not hide. 'Cause

Su - gar - pie hon - ey bunch, you know that I'm
Su - gar - pie hon - ey bunch, do an - y - thing you

weak for you. _ Can't help my - self, _____
ask me to. _ Can't help my - self, _____

Repeat and Fade

I love _ you and no - bod - y else.
I want _ you and no - bod - y else.

I'll Be There

Words and Music by BERRY GORDY, HAL DAVIS,
WILLIE HUTCH and BOB WEST

Moderately

You and I   must make   a pact.   We must bring   sal - va - tion back. _____

Where there is   love, _____   I'll ___ be there.

(I'll   be there.) _

I'll reach out   my hand   to you,

I'll be there to pro - tect ___ you

I'll have faith   in

with an un - sel - fish love ___

I Hear a Symphony

Words and Music by EDWARD HOLLAND,
LAMONT DOZIER and BRIAN HOLLAND

I Heard It Through the Grapevine

Words and Music by NORMAN WHITFIELD
and BARRETT STRONG

I Second That Emotion

Words and Music by WILLIAM "SMOKEY" ROBINSON
and ALFRED CLEVELAND

I Want You Back

Words and Music by FREDDIE PERREN, ALPHONSO MIZELL,
BERRY GORDY and DEKE RICHARDS

I'm Losing You
(I Know)

Words and Music by CORNELIUS GRANT,
NORMAN WHITFIELD and EDWARD HOLLAND

If I Were Your Woman

Words and Music by LAVERNE WARE,
PAM SAWYER and CLAY McMURRAY

D.S. al Coda

It's the Same Old Song

Words and Music by EDWARD HOLLAND,
LAMONT DOZIER and BRIAN HOLLAND

bring __ sweet mem - o - ries of a ten - der love __ that
hear - ing the part __ that used to touch our heart

used to be. __ Now it's the } same old __ song, __ but with a
break - ing up, nev - er. It's the }

dif - f'rent mean - ing since - a you been gone. __ Now it's the same, same old __

song, but with a dif - f'rent mean - ing since you been gone. __

To Coda

Just My Imagination
(Running Away with Me)

Words and Music by NORMAN WHITFIELD
and BARRETT STRONG

Let's Get It On

Words and Music by MARVIN GAYE
and ED TOWNSEND

Slow Soul beat

I've been real-ly try - in', ba - by, try-in' to hold _ back this feel-

in' for so _ long. And if you feel like _ I feel, _ ba-by,

then come on, _ on, _ come on. Ooh, _ let's get it on. Ow, _____

Lookin' through the Windows

Words and Music by
CLIFTON DAVIS

Love Is Like an Itching in My Heart

Words and Music by EDWARD HOLLAND,
LAMONT DOZIER and BRIAN HOLLAND

The Love You Save

Words and Music by BERRY GORDY, ALPHONSO MIZELL,
FREDDIE PERREN and DENNIS LUSSIER

Maybe Tomorrow

Words and Music by BERRY GORDY, ALPHONSO J. MIZELL,
FREDERICK J. PERREN and DENNIS LUSSIER

the way you do, ba - by. 'Cause,

Chorus:

you are the book that I read each day.__ You are the song__ that I sing.__

__ Gon-na sing it to__ you. You are the four sea-sons of my life.__ But

may - be to - mor - row__ you'll change your__ mind,__ girl. May - be to - mor - row, you'll come

Mercy, Mercy Me
(The Ecology)

Words and Music by
MARVIN GAYE

More Love

Words and Music by
WILLIAM "SMOKEY" ROBINSON

Verse 2:
This is no fiction, this no act,
This is real, it's a fact.
I'll always belong only to you,
And each day I'll be living to
Make sure I'm giving you ... *(To Chorus:)*

Verse 3:
As we grow older, no need to fear,
'Cause when you need me I'll be here.
I'll be beside you every step of the way.
A heart that's truthful, and is keeping it youthful
With ... *(To Chorus:)*

Money
(That's What I Want)

Words and Music by BERRY GORDY
and JANIE BRADFORD

Moderate rock

1. The best___ things in life are free,___
2. Your love - in' give me a thrill,___
3. 4. Mon - ey don't get ev - 'ry thing it's true,___

Never Can Say Goodbye

Words and Music by
CLIFTON DAVIS

Nev-er can ___ say good-bye, ___ no, ___ no, no, no. I

nev-er can ___ say good-bye. ___

E - ven
Ev - 'ry
I keep

though the pain and heart - ache ___ seem to fol-low me wher-ev-er I go, ___ though I
time I think I've had ___ e - nough and start head - ing for the door, ___ there's a
think - in' that our prob - lems ___ soon are all gon - na work out, ___ but there's that

My Girl

Words and Music by WILLIAM "SMOKEY" ROBINSON
and RONALD WHITE

I've got sun-shine

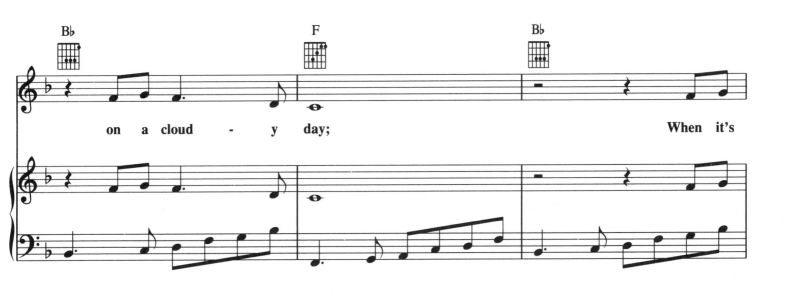

on a cloud - y day;   When it's

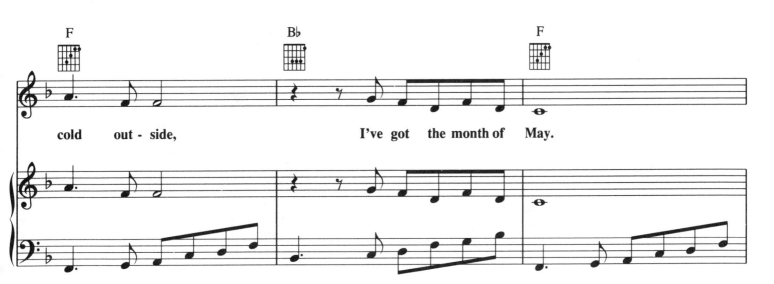

cold out - side,   I've got the month of May.

My Guy

Words and Music by
WILLIAM "SMOKEY" ROBINSON

My World Is Empty Without You

Words and Music by EDWARD HOLLAND,
LAMONT DOZIER and BRIAN HOLLAND

Nowhere to Run

Words and Music by LAMONT DOZIER,
BRIAN HOLLAND and EDDIE HOLLAND

Ooo Baby Baby

Words and Music by WILLIAM "SMOKEY" ROBINSON
and WARREN MOORE

Sail On

Words and Music by
LIONEL RICHIE

sail on hon-ey, good times__ nev-er
Sail on su-gar, good times__ nev-er

felt so_good.__
felt so_good.__

Sail on.

Repeat and Fade

Papa Was a Rollin' Stone

Words and Music by NORMAN WHITFIELD
and BARRETT STRONG

1. that was the day __ that my dad - dy died. __

Ma - ma, I'm de - pend - ing on you to tell me the truth. __

2. I __ *Spoken: Mama just hung her head and said, "Son,*

Pa - pa was a roll - in' stone." __ Wher - ev - er he laid his hat

was his home. __ And when he died, __ all __ he __ left us was a -

A Place In the Sun

Words and Music by RONALD MILLER
and BRYAN WELLS

Repeat and Fade

Reach Out and Touch
(Somebody's Hand)

Words and Music by NICKOLAS ASHFORD
and VALERIE SIMPSON

Shake Me, Wake Me
(When It's Over)

Words and Music by EDWARD HOLLAND,
LAMONT DOZIER and BRIAN HOLLAND

Gospel Rock

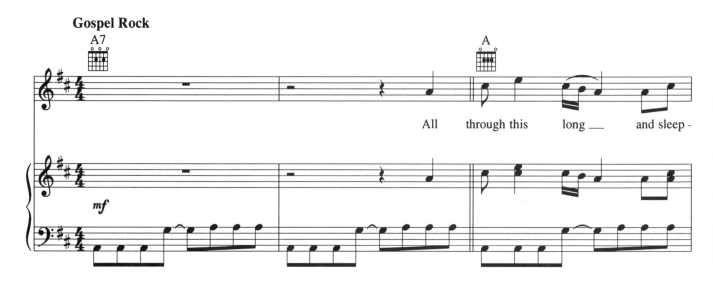

less night, I hear my neigh - bors talk - ing, _____ Say - ing that

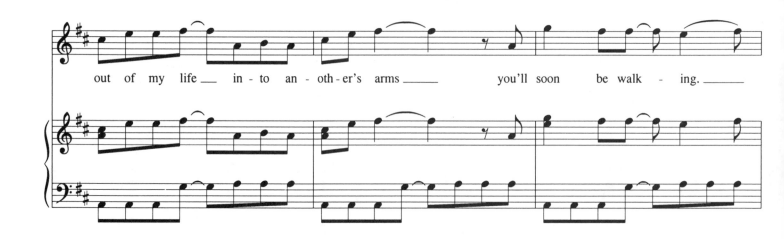

out of my life ___ in - to an - oth - er's arms _____ you'll soon be walk - ing. _____

Solo ends

Restlessly, _____ I pace the floor, _____ respect to my neighbors' criticize, _____ what a fool I am _____ not to realize _____ you don't want me by ___ your side. ___ Wipe the

Shop Around

Words and Music by BERRY GORDY
and WILLIAM "SMOKEY" ROBINSON

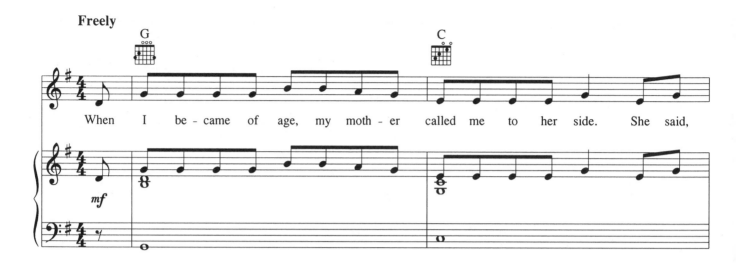

When I be-came of age, my moth-er called me to her side. She said,

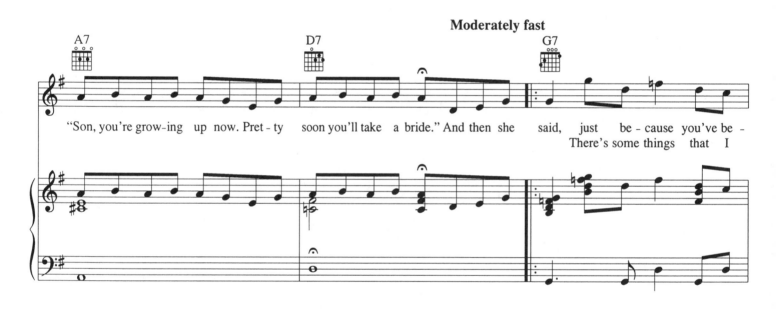

"Son, you're grow-ing up now. Pret-ty soon you'll take a bride." And then she said, just be-cause you've be-
There's some things that I

come a young man now, there's still some things that you
want you to know now. Just as sure as the

Somebody's Watching Me

Words and Music by
ROCKWELL

(Spoken:) *I'm just an av-erage man,*   *with an av-erage life.*   *I work from nine to five;___*
2.3.(See additional lyric)

hey hell, I pay the price.___   *All I want is to be left a-lone___*

1. 3. Tell me, is it just a dream? tricks on me? 3. just a dream?
2. 4. 6. Who's play-ing 4. 6. tricks on me?
5. Tell me who 5. can it be?

Verse 2:
When I come home at night,
I bolt the door real tight.
People call me on the phone I'm trying to avoid.
Well, can the people on T.V. see me,
Or am I just paranoid?

Verse 3:
When I'm in the shower,
I'm afraid to wash my hair,
'Cause I might open my eyes
And find someone standing there.
People say I'm crazy,
Just a little touched.
But maybe showers remind me of
"Psycho" too much.
That's why...
(To Chorus:)

Smiling Faces Sometimes

Words and Music by NORMAN WHITFIELD
and BARRETT STRONG

Someday We'll Be Together

Words and Music by JACKEY BEAVERS,
JOHNNY BRISTOL and HARVEY FUQUA

Standing in the Shadows of Love

Words and Music by EDWARD HOLLAND,
LAMONT DOZIER and BRIAN HOLLAND

Still

Words and Music by
LIONEL RICHIE

Stop! In the Name of Love

Words and Music by LAMONT DOZIER,
BRIAN HOLLAND and EDWARD HOLLAND

Take a Look Around

Words and Music by BARRETT STRONG
and NORMAN WHITFIELD

Time Will Reveal

Words and Music by BUNNY DeBARGE
and ELDRA DeBARGE

Three Times a Lady

Words and Music by
LIONEL RICHIE

Slowly

Thanks for the times that you've giv - en me. ___ The mem - 'ries ___ are all ___ in my mind. ___

258

You're once,
twice, three times _____ a la-dy, _____ and I

love _____ you, _____ I love _

you.

War

Words and Music by NORMAN WHITFIELD
and BARRETT STRONG

War means tears ___ in thou - sands of mo-thers' eyes ___ when their

Fade on last repeat

sons go out to fight _ and lose _ their ___ lives. ___ I said

Additional Lyrics

2. War, uh! What is it good for? Absolutely nothing; say it again;
   War, uh! What is it good for? Absolutely nothing.
   War, it's nothing but a heartbreaker; War, friend only to the undertaker.
   War is an enemy to all mankind. The thought of war blows my mind.
   War has caused unrest within the younger generation;
   Induction then destruction, who wants to die? Ah
   War, uh um; What is it good for? You tell me nothing, um!
   War, uh! What is it good for? Absolutely nothing.
   Good God, war, it's nothing but a heartbreaker;
   War, friend only to the undertaker;

3. Wars have shattered many a young man's dreams;
   Made him disabled, bitter and mean.
   Life is much too short and precious to spend fighting wars each day.
   War can't give life, it can only take it away. Ah
   War, Uh um! What is it good for? Absolutely nothing, um.
   War, good God almighty, listen, what is it good for? Absolutely nothing, yeah.
   War, it's nothing but a heartbreaker; War, friend only to the undertaker.
   Peace, love and understanding, tell me is there no place for them today?
   They say we must fight to keep our freedom, but Lord knows it's gotta be a better way.
   I say war, uh um, yeah, yeah. What is it good for? Absolutely nothing; say it again;
   War, yea, yea, yea, yea, what is it good for? Absolutely nothing; say it again;
   War, nothing but a heartbreaker; What is it good for? Friend only to the undertaker.....
   (Fade)

Touch Me in the Morning

Words and Music by RONALD MILLER
and MICHAEL MASSER

(A Bass)

If I've got to be strong, don't you know I need to have to-night when you're gone? Till you go I need to

1. (Spoken or Sung:) lie here and think a - bout, _____ the last time that you'll) Touch me in the

2. hold you un - til the time, your hands reach out and touch me in the

Duet: { morn - ing.
Morn-ings were blue and gold and we could feel one an-oth - er liv - ing.
Then just walk a -

The Tracks of My Tears

Words and Music by WILLIAM "SMOKEY" ROBINSON,
WARREN MOORE and MARVIN TARPLIN

Way Over There

Words and Music by WILLIAM "SMOKEY" ROBINSON
and BERRY GORDY

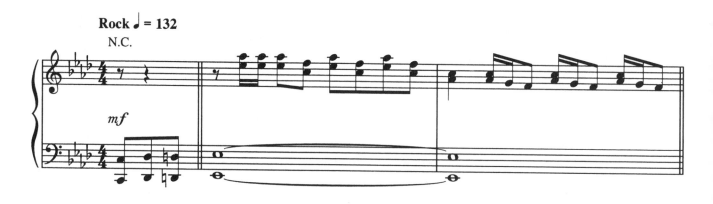

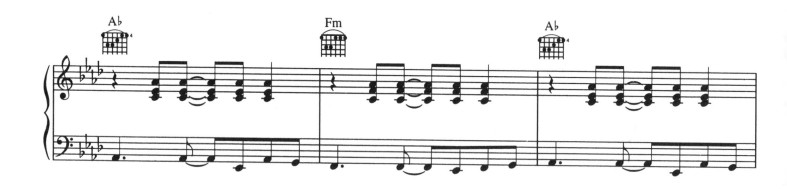

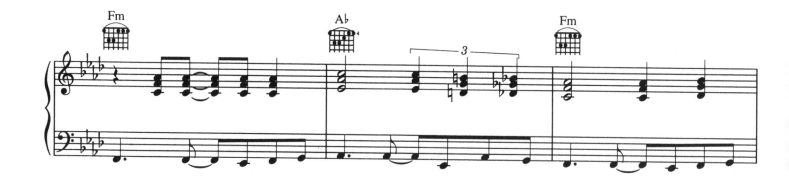

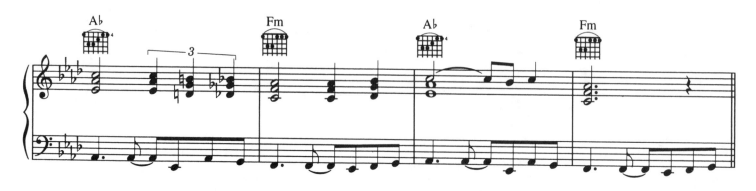

Verse 2 & 3:
They tell me that the river's too deep and it's much too wide.
"Boy, you can't get over to the other side."
But they don't know I got to get there and hold her in my arms
Just one more time, like I did before when she was mine, all mine.
'Cause I can hear her saying, "Come to me, baby."
I'm on my way.
"Come to me, baby."
I'm gonna stay.
"I'm gonna get to you."
No matter what I have to do.

The Way You Do the Things You Do

Words and Music by WILLIAM "SMOKEY" ROBINSON
and ROBERT ROGERS

What's Going On

Words and Music by MARVIN GAYE,
AL CLEVELAND and RENALDO BENSON

ya, ya, ya.

I, yi, yi, yi, yi, yi, ya, ya, ya, ya, ya.

A/B

Be, doot, de, doot; Be, be, be, doot; Be be, be, doot;

Repeat and Fade

Bu, doot, be, be, be, doot; Be be, be, be, be, doot. Ooh,

Where Did Our Love Go

Words and Music by BRIAN HOLLAND,
LAMONT DOZIER and EDWARD HOLLAND

You're All I Need to Get By

Words and Music by NICKOLAS ASHFORD
and VALERIE SIMPSON

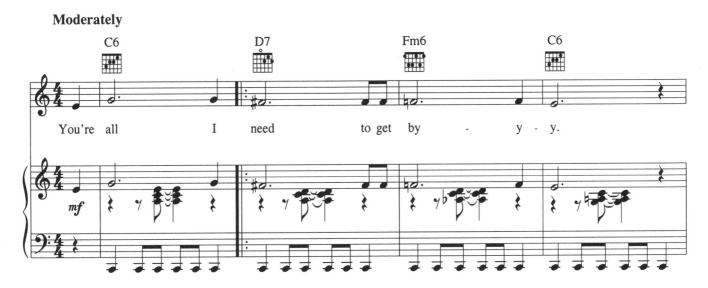

You Can't Hurry Love

Words and Music by EDWARD HOLLAND,
LAMONT DOZIER and BRIAN HOLLAND

You Keep Me Hangin' On

Words and Music by EDWARD HOLLAND,
LAMONT DOZIER and BRIAN HOLLAND

You've Really Got a Hold on Me

Words and Music by
WILLIAM "SMOKEY" ROBINSON

Slowly

I don't___ like you,___ but I___ love you;
I don't___ want you,___ but I___ need you;
I wan - na leave you,___ don't wan - na stay here;

Seems that I'm al - ways___ think - ing of you.___
Don't wan - na kiss you,___ but I___ need to.___
Don't wan - na spend___ an - oth - er day here.___

You've Made Me So Very Happy

Words and Music by BERRY GORDY, FRANK E. WILSON,
BRENDA HOLLOWAY and PATRICE HOLLOWAY

I'm so in love with you ____ All I ev-er want to do _ is thank you ba - by,

thank you, ba - by!

You made me _ so _ ver - y hap-py.